VIRGINIA TEST PREP
Practice Test Book
SOL Mathematics
Grade 3

© 2018 by V. Hawas

All rights reserved. No part of this book may be reproduced or transmitted in any form or by any means, electronic, mechanical, photocopying, recording, or otherwise without prior written permission.

ISBN 978-1725634244

TEST MASTER PRESS

www.testmasterpress.com

Created by Test Master Press   www.testmasterpress.com

CONTENTS

Introduction	**4**
SOL Mathematics: Mini-Tests	**5**
Mini-Test 1	5
Mini-Test 2	13
SOL Mathematics: Practice Test 1	**21**
Section 1	21
Section 2	33
SOL Mathematics: Practice Test 2	**46**
Section 1	46
Section 2	58
SOL Mathematics: Practice Test 3	**70**
Section 1	70
Section 2	82
SOL Mathematics: Practice Test 4	**94**
Section 1	94
Section 2	106
Answer Key	**121**
Mini-Test 1	122
Mini-Test 2	124
Practice Test 1, Section 1	125
Practice Test 1, Section 2	127
Practice Test 2, Section 1	129
Practice Test 2, Section 2	130
Practice Test 3, Section 1	131
Practice Test 3, Section 2	133
Practice Test 4, Section 1	134
Practice Test 4, Section 2	135

INTRODUCTION
For Parents, Teachers, and Tutors

About the SOL Mathematics Assessments

Students will be assessed each year by taking the SOL Mathematics assessments. This practice test book will prepare students for the assessments. It contains two mini-tests that will introduce students to the types of tasks they will need to complete. This is followed by four full-length practice tests similar to the real SOL Mathematics tests.

About the Standards of Learning

In 2016, the state of Virginia adopted new *Standards of Learning*. The *Standards of Learning* describe what students are expected to know. Student learning throughout the year is based on these standards, and all the questions on the SOL Mathematics assessments cover these standards. All the exercises and questions in this book cover the *Standards of Learning* introduced in 2016.

Types of Tasks on the SOL Mathematics Assessments

The SOL Mathematics tests are taken online as computer adaptive tests. These tests contain several question types, including technology-enhanced items. The questions types are described below.

- Multiple-choice – students select the one correct answer from four possible options.
- Fill-in-the-blank – students write a number or word in a blank space.
- Hot spot – students select one or more elements. These questions could involve selecting items, shading parts of a figure, completing a graph, or marking points on a number line.
- Drag and drop – students drag one or more draggers to drop zones. Draggers could be numbers, words, or symbols. These questions could involve writing fractions, completing an equation, placing numbers in order, or labeling items.

This practice test book contains multiple-choice questions and questions with similar formats to the technology-enhanced items. To ensure that students develop strong mathematics skills, this book also contains written answer questions. These questions will give students the opportunity to describe mathematics concepts and explain their thinking.

Taking the Tests

The first two mini-tests introduce students to the assessments with 10 questions that cover all the common question types. These short tests will allow students to become familiar with the types of questions they will encounter before moving on to longer tests. These shorter tests may also be used as guided instruction before allowing students to complete the assessments on their own.

The mini-tests are followed by four full-length practice tests. These have the same question types and assess the same skills as the real SOL Mathematics tests. To ensure that all skills are covered, the practice tests are longer than the actual SOL tests and have 40 questions each instead of 32. Just like the real SOL tests, the practice tests are divided into two sections. Students can complete the two sections on the same day or on different days, but should have a break between sect ions.

SOL Mathematics

Grade 3

Mini-Test 1

Instructions

Read each question carefully. For each multiple-choice question, fill in the circle for the correct answer. For other types of questions, follow the directions given in the question.

You may use a ruler to help you answer questions. You may not use a calculator on this test.

1 Which fraction is represented by point *Y*?

- Ⓐ $\frac{1}{3}$
- Ⓑ $\frac{1}{4}$
- Ⓒ $\frac{1}{5}$
- Ⓓ $\frac{1}{8}$

2 Sandra arrived at her friend's house at 8:00 a.m. She stayed at her friend's house for 7 hours. What time did Sandra leave her friend's house?

- Ⓐ 2:00 p.m.
- Ⓑ 3:00 p.m.
- Ⓒ 4:00 p.m.
- Ⓓ 5:00 p.m.

3   Karisa wants to determine how much water the dog bowl below can hold. Which measurement would Karisa be best to find?

- Ⓐ Volume
- Ⓑ Weight
- Ⓒ Height
- Ⓓ Length

4   Place the names of the shapes below in order from the least sides to the most sides.

octagon   triangle   hexagon   pentagon

Least   Triangle

        hexagon

        octagon

Most   pentagon

5   Select **all** the equations that will be true if the number 8 is placed in the empty box.

☒   6 × ☐ = 48

☑   8 × ☐ = 56

☒   9 × ☐ = 72

☒   24 ÷ ☐ = 4

☑   40 ÷ ☐ = 5

☑   64 ÷ ☐ = 8

6   Plot the four fractions listed below on the number line.

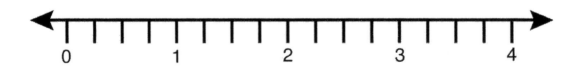

7 Sam kept a record of the types of movies each customer in his store rented. Sam made the table below to show the results.

Type of Movie	Number of Rentals
Action	12
Comedy	14
Drama	8
Science fiction	18

Use the information in the table to complete the graph below.

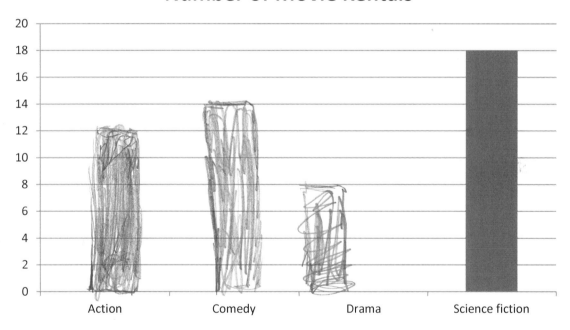

8 Hannah sorts the figures below into those that are quadrilaterals and those that are triangles.

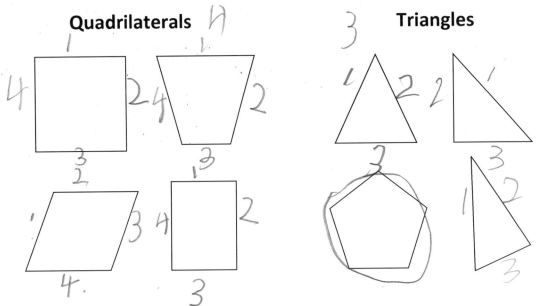

Circle the shape above that Hannah has sorted incorrectly. On the lines below, explain why the shape is sorted incorrectly.

That shape has 5 sides

9. Emilio wants to create a vegetable garden with the shape shown below. On the diagram below, write the numbers in the boxes to show the missing dimensions.

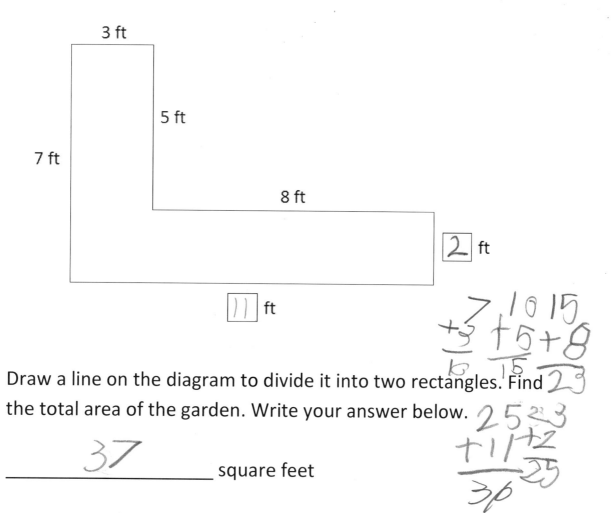

Draw a line on the diagram to divide it into two rectangles. Find the total area of the garden. Write your answer below.

_____37_____ square feet

Find the perimeter of the garden. Write your answer below.

_____36_____ feet

10 An Italian restaurant sells four types of meals. The owner made this graph to show how many meals of each type were sold one night.

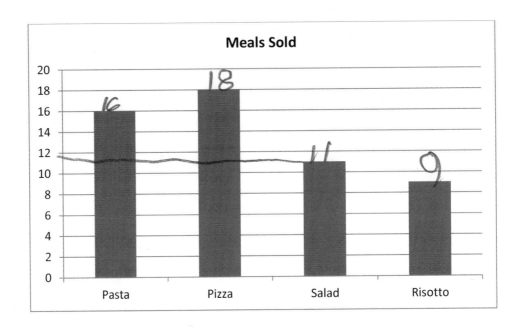

According to the graph, which statement is true?

- Ⓐ The store sold more pizza meals than salad and risotto meals combined.
- Ⓑ The store sold twice as many pizza meals as risotto meals.
- Ⓒ The store sold more pasta meals than any other type of meal.
- Ⓓ The store sold half as many salad meals as pasta meals.

END OF PRACTICE SET

SOL Mathematics

Grade 3

Mini-Test 2

Instructions

Read each question carefully. For each multiple-choice question, fill in the circle for the correct answer. For other types of questions, follow the directions given in the question.

You may use a ruler to help you answer questions. You may not use a calculator on this test.

1. Ryan's basketball team scored 74 points in a match. The team won the match by 9 points. How many points did the other team score?

- Ⓐ 81
- Ⓑ 83
- Ⓒ 65
- Ⓓ 67

2. Andy is learning to speak French. Andy learns 5 new words every day. Complete the table below to show how many words Andy has learned in all after each day.

Number of Days	Number of Words Learned
1 × 5	5
2 × 5	10
3 × 5	15
4 × 5	20
5 × 5	25

3   Anton looked at the clock below.

Which of the following is closest to the time shown on the clock?
Ⓐ   6:20
Ⓑ   4:30
Ⓒ   4:45
Ⓓ   9:00

4   Look at the shapes below. Circle the **two** shapes that appear to be congruent.

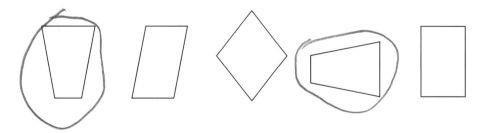

5 Select **all** the fractions that are equivalent to the shaded area of the circle below.

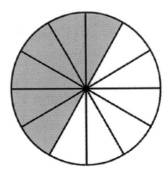

☐ $\frac{6}{1}$

☑ $\frac{1}{2}$

☑ $\frac{6}{12}$

☐ $\frac{2}{4}$

☐ $\frac{8}{4}$

☐ $\frac{2}{3}$

6   Jo has 18 star-shaped stickers. He places them in 3 even rows. Which of these shows how many stickers are in each row?

Ⓐ

Ⓑ

Ⓒ

Ⓓ

7   Simon had $896 in his savings account. He spent $179 on car repairs. How much money does Simon have left? Write your answer below.

$ _____

8 Alex started the number pattern below. Continue the pattern by writing the next four numbers on the lines below.

6, 10, 14, 18, 22, _28_, _34_, _40_, _46_

Will all the numbers in the pattern be even? Explain why or why not.

_____

_____

_____

_____

9   The pictograph below shows how long Tammy spent at the computer each week day.

Monday	🖥🖥🖥🖥
Tuesday	🖥🖥🖥🖥🖥🖥
Wednesday	🖥🖥🖥🖥🖥
Thursday	🖥🖥🖥
Friday	🖥🖥

Each 🖥 means 10 minutes.

On which day did Tammy spend the least time at the computer? Write your answer below.

Friday

How many minutes did Tammy spend at the computer on Monday? Write your answer below.

40 minutes

How much more time did Tammy spend at the computer on Tuesday than Thursday? Write your answer below.

60 minutes

10 Look at the shaded figure below.

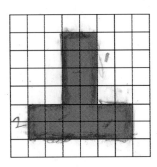

Divide the figure into two rectangles. Write the dimensions of the two rectangles below.

Rectangle 1: _____ by _____ units

Rectangle 2: _____ by _____ units

What is the total area of the shaded figure? Write your answer below.

_____ square units

END OF PRACTICE SET

SOL Mathematics

Grade 3

Practice Test 1

Section 1

Instructions

Read each question carefully. For each multiple-choice question, fill in the circle for the correct answer. For other types of questions, follow the directions given in the question.

You may use a ruler to help you answer questions. You may not use a calculator on this test.

1   Mario buys screws in packets of 6.

If Mario counts the screws in groups of 6, which of these numbers would he count? Circle **all** the numbers he would count.

(16)   (18)   22   (26)

(30)   (36)   40   (42)

2   The graph shows how long Jason studied for one week.

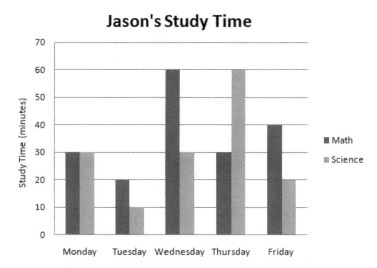

On what day did Jason study science for 30 minutes less than math? Write your answer below.

Monday

3   Select **all** the fractions below that are equal to 4.

☒ $\frac{2}{8}$

☒ $\frac{8}{4}$

☐ $\frac{15}{5}$

☒ $\frac{4}{1}$

☒ $\frac{12}{3}$

4   Sally is making a pictograph to show how many students are in grade 3, grade 4, and grade 5.

Grade 3	☺☺☺☺☺☺☺☺☺☺
Grade 4	☺☺☺☺☺☺☺☺☺☺☺☺
Grade 5	

☺ = 5 students

There are 65 students in grade 5. Which of these should Sally use to represent 65 students?

5 Damon rode 3 miles to school every morning, and 3 miles back home each afternoon. How many miles would he ride in 5 days?

Ⓐ 15 miles

Ⓑ 30 miles

Ⓒ 45 miles

Ⓓ 60 miles

6 Ribbon costs $4 per yard. Allie buys 16 yards of ribbon. Which number sentence could be used to find the total cost of the ribbon, *c*, in dollars?

Ⓐ $16 + 4 = c$

Ⓑ $16 - 4 = c$

Ⓒ $16 \times 4 = c$

Ⓓ $16 \div 4 = c$

7 Allen's car has traveled 5,648 miles since it was new. What is this number rounded to the nearest hundred? Write your answer below.

_____

8   The school library has 1,532 fiction books, 1,609 non-fiction books, and 1,239 children's books. Complete the number sentence by rounding each number to the nearest hundred and then completing the addition.

1,500 + ___1,600___ + ___1,200___ = ___4,300___

9   There are 157 male students and 165 female students at Ella's school. How many students are there in all?

   Ⓐ 322
   Ⓑ 312
   Ⓒ 222
   ● 212

10 Plot the fraction $1\frac{1}{4}$ on the number line below.

11   Look at the group of numbers below. Round each number to the nearest ten. Write your answers below.

108 _100_   864 _800_

87   _90_   196 _200_

282 _200_   35   _30_

981 _900_   773 _700_

On the lines below, explain how you decided whether to round each number up or down.

down

12 During the baseball season, Marvin's team won 5 games and lost 14 games.

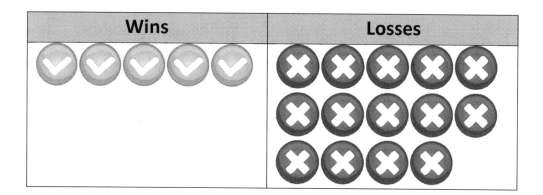

What fraction of the total games did the team win? Write your answer below.

13 Shade the models below to show $\frac{3}{10}$ and $\frac{1}{5}$.

$\frac{3}{10}$

$\frac{1}{5}$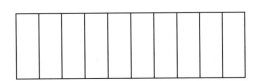

Place one of the symbols below in the number sentence to compare the fractions $\frac{3}{10}$ and $\frac{1}{5}$.

<, >, =

$\frac{3}{10}$ ☐ $\frac{1}{5}$

On the lines below, explain how the models helped you find the answer.

_____

_____

_____

_____

14 Look at the pattern below.

$$16, 19, 22, 25, 28, 31, \_\_\_\_$$

Write an expression that can be used to find the next number in the pattern. Use *x* to represent the last number in the pattern.

Expression _____

Use the expression to find the next number in the pattern.

Answer _____

Use the expression to find the number that would come after 112.

Answer _____

15 What temperature is shown on the thermometer below? Write your answer on the line below.

_____ °C

16 A company has 4 salespersons. Each salesperson works 40 hours each week. How many hours do all the salespeople work in all?

Ⓐ   80 hours

Ⓑ   120 hours

Ⓒ   160 hours

Ⓓ   240 hours

17 A dance class usually has 30 students in it. On Monday, there were 6 students missing from the class and 2 extra students visiting the class. Write the correct symbols in the boxes to complete the number sentence that shows how many students were in the class on Monday. Then complete the calculation.

$$30 \boxed{-} 6 \boxed{+} 2 = \boxed{26}$$

18 There were 17,856 people living in Eastwood in 2009. What is the value of the digit 8 in 17,856?

- Ⓐ　Eight hundred
- Ⓑ　Eight thousand
- Ⓒ　Eighty thousand
- Ⓓ　Eighty

19 What fraction of the model is shaded?

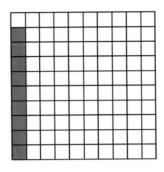

- Ⓐ $\frac{1}{9}$
- Ⓑ $\frac{9}{10}$
- Ⓒ $\frac{9}{91}$
- Ⓓ $\frac{9}{100}$

20 Which of the following is another way to write quarter past five?

- Ⓐ 5:25
- Ⓑ 5:30
- Ⓒ 5:45
- Ⓓ 5:15

END OF PRACTICE SET

SOL Mathematics

Grade 3

Practice Test 1

Section 2

Instructions

Read each question carefully. For each multiple-choice question, fill in the circle for the correct answer. For other types of questions, follow the directions given in the question.

You may use a ruler to help you answer questions. You may not use a calculator on this test.

1. Which of these shows one way to divide a hexagon into two congruent shapes?

Ⓐ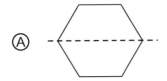

Ⓑ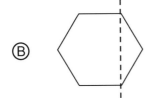

Ⓒ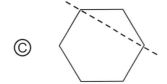

Ⓓ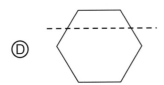

2. There were some people on a bus. After a stop, there were 4 times as many people on the bus. If there were 36 people on the bus after the stop, which equation can be used to find how many people, *p*, were on the bus to start with?

Ⓐ $p \times 4 = 36$

Ⓑ $p \div 4 = 36$

Ⓒ $p + 4 = 36$

Ⓓ $p - 4 = 36$

3   Inga made the design below.

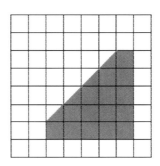

Each square measures 1 square centimeter. What is the area of the shaded part of the design?

- Ⓐ   16 square centimeters
- Ⓑ   17 square centimeters
- Ⓒ   18 square centimeters
- Ⓓ   19 square centimeters

4   Kyle drove for 4 hours. How many minutes did Kyle drive for?

- Ⓐ   180 minutes
- Ⓑ   240 minutes
- Ⓒ   320 minutes
- Ⓓ   400 minutes

5   Which measurement is the best estimate of the length of a fire engine?

- Ⓐ   10 inches
- Ⓑ   10 centimeters
- Ⓒ   10 feet
- Ⓓ   10 meters

6   Look at the number pattern below.

48, 42, 36, 30, 24, …

If the pattern continues, what two numbers will come next?

- Ⓐ   22, 20
- Ⓑ   30, 36
- Ⓒ   20, 16
- Ⓓ   18, 12

7 Rita made the pictograph below to show how many cans each class collected for a food drive.

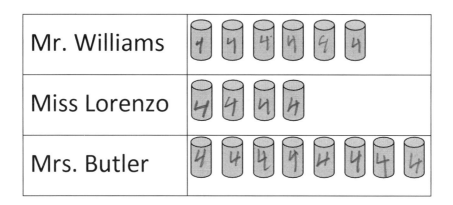

= 4 cans

How many cans did Miss Lorenzo's class collect? Write your answer below.

___16___ cans

8 What is the perimeter of the rectangle below?

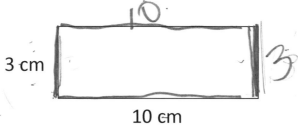

- Ⓐ 13 cm
- Ⓑ 30 cm
- Ⓒ 26 cm
- Ⓓ 60 cm

9 Lei jogs for the same number of minutes every day. The table shows how far she jogs in total after 1, 2, 3, and 4 days. Complete the table to show how many minutes Lei jogs for in total after 5, 6, and 7 days.

Number of Days	Number of Minutes
1	15
2	30
3	45
4	60
5	
6	
7	

10 The thermometer below shows the temperature at 5 p.m. on Tuesday.

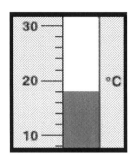

By 10 p.m. on Tuesday, the temperature had dropped by 4°C. Show the temperate at 10 p.m. on Tuesday on the thermometer below.

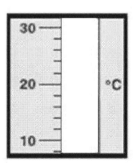

11 Round 8,782 to the nearest ten and the nearest hundred. Write your answers on the lines below.

Nearest ten _____

Nearest hundred _____

On the lines below, explain how you worked out whether to round the number up or down in each case.

_____

_____

_____

_____

_____

12 Harris saved $48 in 8 weeks. He saved the same amount of money each week. How much did Harris save each week? Write your answer below.

$ _____

13 Joy got on a train at 1:30 p.m. Joy got off the train at 4:30 p.m. For how many minutes was Joy on the train? Write your answer below.

_____ minutes

14 Shade the fractions $\frac{1}{2}$ and $\frac{2}{4}$ on the fraction models below.

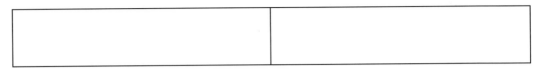

Shade the fraction model below to show another fraction equivalent to $\frac{1}{2}$ and $\frac{2}{4}$. Write the fraction on the line below.

Fraction _____

15 What is the area of the rectangle shown on the grid below? Write your answer below.

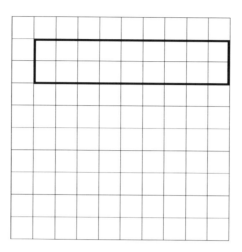

_____ square units

On the grid below, draw a rectangle with the same area but a different perimeter.

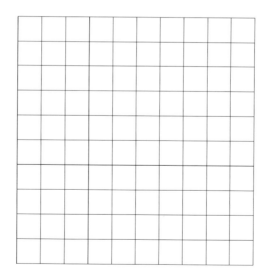

16 Margaret surveyed students about who they would vote for in a class election. Davis made the graph below to show the results.

Davis	☺☺☺☺
Bobby	
Inga	☺☺☺☺☺☺☺

Each ☺ means 2 students.

In the survey, 8 students said they would vote for Bobby. How many symbols should Margaret use to show 8 votes?

Ⓐ   8

Ⓑ   4

Ⓒ   2

Ⓓ   16

17 Kim is 63 inches tall. Chelsea is 4 inches taller than Kim. Vicky is 3 inches shorter than Chelsea. Which expression could be used to find Vicky's height, in inches?

Ⓐ   63 – 4 – 3

Ⓑ   63 + 4 + 3

Ⓒ   63 – 4 + 3

Ⓓ   63 + 4 – 3

18   Miss Jenkins received wages of $655. She saved $80 of her wages and spent the rest. How much money did Miss Jenkins spend? Write your answer below.

$ _____

19   Bananas sell for $3 per pound. Stacey buys 9 pounds of bananas. How much would the bananas cost?
   Ⓐ $12
   Ⓑ $27
   Ⓒ $18
   Ⓓ $21

20   A picture frame is 8 inches wide and 5 inches high. What is the perimeter of the frame?
   Ⓐ   26 inches
   Ⓑ   32 inches
   Ⓒ   20 inches
   Ⓓ   40 inches

END OF PRACTICE SET

SOL Mathematics

Grade 3

Practice Test 2

Section 1

Instructions

Read each question carefully. For each multiple-choice question, fill in the circle for the correct answer. For other types of questions, follow the directions given in the question.

You may use a ruler to help you answer questions. You may not use a calculator on this test.

1. Sara walked around the four outside edges of a football field. If Sara recorded the total distance she walked, what would Sara have determined?

   Ⓐ The area of the football field

   Ⓑ The volume of the football field

   Ⓒ The perimeter of the football field

   Ⓓ The surface area of the football field

2. A piece of note paper has side lengths of 12 centimeters. What is the area of the piece of note paper?

   Ⓐ 48 square centimeters

   Ⓑ 72 square centimeters

   Ⓒ 120 square centimeters

   Ⓓ 144 square centimeters

3 Leah made 500 cakes of soap to sell at a fair. She sold 182 cakes of soap on Saturday. Then she sold 218 cakes of soap on Sunday. Choose the **two** expressions that can be used to find how many cakes of soap she had left.

☐ 500 + 182 + 218

☐ 500 + 182 − 218

☐ 500 − 182 − 218

☐ 500 − (182 + 218)

☐ 500 − (218 − 182)

☐ 500 + (218 − 182)

4 Michael drove 1,285 miles during a vacation. How far did Michael drive to the nearest hundred and the nearest ten? Write your answers below.

Nearest hundred: _____ miles

Nearest ten: _____ miles

5   Donna has 18 roses. She wants to put the roses into vases so that each vase has the same number of roses, with no roses left over.

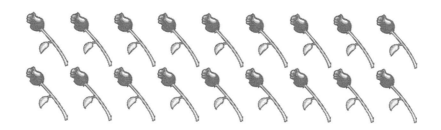

How many roses could Donna put in each vase?

Ⓐ   4

Ⓑ   5

Ⓒ   6

Ⓓ   8

6   Stevie had $1.45. She bought a drink for $1.20. Stevie was given one coin as change. Which coin should Stevie have been given?

Ⓐ   A dime

Ⓑ   A penny

Ⓒ   A quarter

Ⓓ   A nickel

7 Look at the shaded figure below.

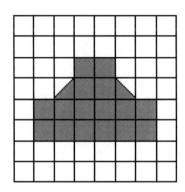

What is the area of the shaded figure?

Ⓐ 17 square units

Ⓑ 16 square units

Ⓒ 18 square units

Ⓓ 24 square units

8 Billy collects pennies and nickels. Billy has 142 pennies and 56 nickels in his coin collection. Which is the best estimate of the total number of coins in Billy's collection?

Ⓐ 150

Ⓑ 180

Ⓒ 200

Ⓓ 250

9 The figure below models the number sentence 6 × 2 = 12.

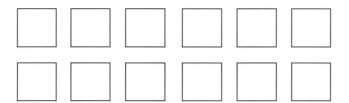

Which number sentence is modeled by the same figure?

Ⓐ 6 ÷ 2 = 3

Ⓑ 36 ÷ 3 = 12

Ⓒ 12 ÷ 6 = 2

Ⓓ 24 ÷ 2 = 12

10 Which numbers make the number sentences below true? Write the numbers in the boxes.

18 × ☐ = 18

18 × ☐ = 0

11 The graph shows how far four students travel to school.

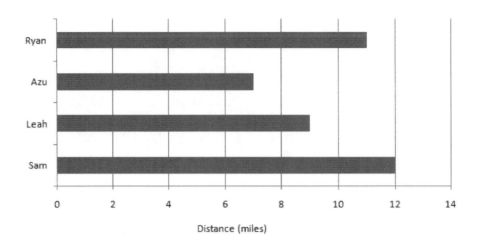

How much farther does Ryan travel than Azu? Write your answer below.

_____ miles

Which two students travel a total of 20 miles? Write your answer below.

_____ and _____

Claudia travels half the distance that Sam travels. How far does Claudia travel? Write your answer below.

_____ miles

12 What is the total area of the shaded portion of the grid?

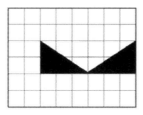

- Ⓐ 3 square units
- Ⓑ 6 square units
- Ⓒ 12 square units
- Ⓓ 16 square units

13 A school play was performed on three nights. The table below shows the number of people that saw the school play each night.

Day	Number of People
Friday	225
Saturday	318
Sunday	290

Which number sentence shows the best estimate of the total number of people who saw the school play?

- Ⓐ 200 + 300 + 200 = 700
- Ⓑ 200 + 300 + 300 = 800
- Ⓒ 200 + 400 + 300 = 900
- Ⓓ 300 + 400 + 300 = 1,000

14 Aaron has quarters and dimes. Aaron's coins are shown below.

Complete the **two** fractions that show the fraction of coins that are quarters.

$$\frac{2}{6} = \frac{\square}{3}$$

15 Which number sentence represents the array shown below?

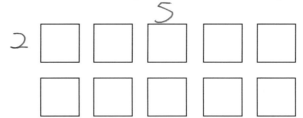

Ⓐ 5 + 2 = 7

Ⓑ 5 × 5 = 25

Ⓒ 5 × 2 = 10

Ⓓ 5 − 2 = 3

16 Plot the fraction $2\frac{3}{4}$ on the number line below.

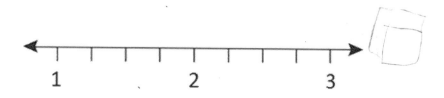

17 The table below shows the different colors of marbles in a bag.

Color	Number of Marbles
Red	5
Green	10
Blue	2
White	3

James selected one marble at random. Match the color with the probability of James selecting that color marble.

Red $\frac{1}{2}$

Green $\frac{1}{10}$

Blue $\frac{3}{20}$

White $\frac{1}{4}$

18   Leah baked 3 pies. She cut each pie into 8 pieces.

How many pieces of pie does Leah have? Write your answer below.

_____24_____ pieces of pie

19   Sarah needs a screwdriver that is smaller than $\frac{3}{8}$ inch. Which screwdriver sizes are less than $\frac{3}{8}$ inch? Select **all** the correct answers.

☐ $\frac{1}{2}$ inch

☐ $\frac{3}{4}$ inch

☐ $\frac{1}{8}$ inch

☐ $\frac{1}{4}$ inch

☐ $\frac{3}{10}$ inch

☐ $\frac{5}{8}$ inch

20 A gift card has a length of 150 mm and a width of 50 mm. Complete the number sentences below to show **two** ways to find the perimeter of the gift card, in millimeters.

_____ + _____ + _____ + _____ = _____

2(_____ + _____) = _____

END OF PRACTICE SET

SOL Mathematics

Grade 3

Practice Test 2

Section 2

Instructions

Read each question carefully. For each multiple-choice question, fill in the circle for the correct answer. For other types of questions, follow the directions given in the question.

You may use a ruler to help you answer questions. You may not use a calculator on this test.

1 Which of these shapes can be divided into two equal triangles by drawing a vertical line down the center?

Ⓐ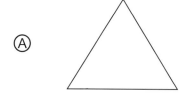

Ⓑ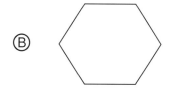

Ⓒ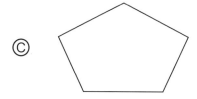

Ⓓ

2 A bookstore sold 40,905 books in May. Which of these is another way to write 40,905?

    Ⓐ   Four thousand nine hundred and five

    Ⓑ   Forty thousand ninety five

    Ⓒ   Four thousand ninety five

    Ⓓ   Forty thousand nine hundred and five

3 Andrew is selling muffins at a bake sale. The table shows the profit he makes by selling 5, 10, 15, and 20 muffins.

Muffins Sold	Profit Made
5	$15
10	$30
15	$45
20	$60

How much profit does Andrew make for selling 1 muffin? Write your answer below.

$_____

How many muffins will Andrew need to sell to make a profit of $150? Write your answer below.

_____ muffins

4 What is the area of the square below? Write your answer below.

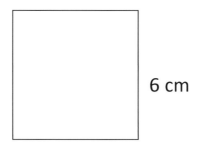

6 cm

_____ cm²

5 Mrs. Bowen cooked dinner for 24 guests. She cooked 3 courses for each guest. Which equation shows how many courses Mrs. Bowen cooked, c?

Ⓐ 24 × 3 = c

Ⓑ 24 + 3 = c

Ⓒ 24 − 3 = c

Ⓓ 24 ÷ 3 = c

6 Which number is greater than 5,167?

Ⓐ 5,096

Ⓑ 5,203

Ⓒ 5,159

Ⓓ 5,164

7 The graph below shows the high temperature in Dallas for five days.

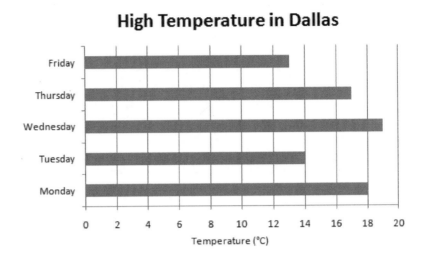

On which day was the high temperature 5°C less than the day with the highest temperature? Write your answer below.

_____

What was the high temperature on Friday? Write your answer below.

_____ °

On Monday, the low temperature was half the high temperature. What was the low temperature on Monday? Write your answer below.

_____ °

8 Shade the model below to show a fraction equivalent to $\frac{6}{8}$.

Write the fraction you shaded in lowest form. Write your answer below.

_____

9 Beads are sold in packets of 6 or packets of 8. Liz needs to buy exactly 30 beads. Which set of packets could Liz buy? Select **all** the correct answers.

☐ 5 packets of 6 beads

☐ 5 packets of 8 beads

☐ 1 packet of 8 beads and 2 packets of 6 beads

☐ 2 packets of 8 beads and 2 packets of 6 beads

☐ 1 packet of 8 beads and 3 packets of 6 beads

☐ 3 packets of 8 beads and 1 packet of 6 beads

10 Joy bought a pair of shorts for $11. Then she bought a scarf for $3. Joy had $18 left. Which equation could be used to find how much money Joy had to start with, *m*?

Ⓐ 18 − 11 + 3 = m

Ⓑ 18 + 11 − 3 = m

Ⓒ m + 11 + 3 = 18

Ⓓ m − 11 − 3 = 18

11 The graph shows how long Jody studied each week day.

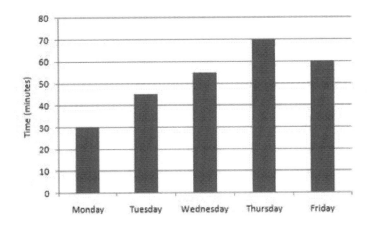

On which day did Jody study for 10 minutes more than the day before?

Ⓐ Tuesday

Ⓑ Wednesday

Ⓒ Thursday

Ⓓ Friday

12. Davis is making a pictograph to show how many letters three students wrote in a month.

Davis	✉✉✉
Bobby	
Inga	✉✉

Each ✉ means 2 letters.

Bobby wrote 8 letters. How many letter symbols should Davis use to show 8 letters?

Ⓐ 8
Ⓑ 4
Ⓒ 2
Ⓓ 16

13. Ray is slicing apples into 8 slices. Complete the table to show how many apple slices Ray will have if he uses 2, 4, and 5 apples.

Number of Apples	Number of Slices
2	
4	
5	

14 Look at the number pattern below. If the pattern continues, which **two** numbers will come next? Write your answers below.

4, 8, 12, 16, 20, _____, _____

15 Which fraction does the shaded model represent?

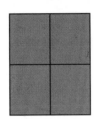 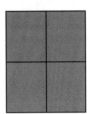 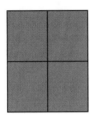  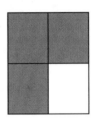

Ⓐ $4\frac{3}{4}$

Ⓑ $4\frac{1}{4}$

Ⓒ $5\frac{3}{4}$

Ⓓ $5\frac{1}{4}$

16 Which fraction model is equivalent to $\frac{1}{2}$?

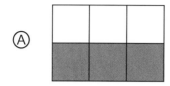

Ⓐ

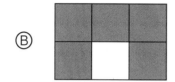

Ⓑ

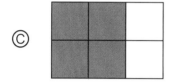

Ⓒ

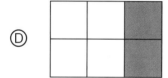

Ⓓ

17 Damien folded the shirts and shorts shown below.

What fraction of the clothes folded were shorts? Write your answer below.

_____

18 David filled the bucket below with water.

About how much water would it take to fill the bucket?

Ⓐ 10 cups

Ⓑ 10 pints

Ⓒ 10 liters

Ⓓ 10 gallons

19 The Walker family drove 182 miles on Saturday. Then they drove 218 miles on Sunday. How many miles did the family travel in all?

Ⓐ 300 miles

Ⓑ 290 miles

Ⓒ 400 miles

Ⓓ 390 miles

20 Rima found the coins shown below when she cleaned out her school bag. How much money did Rima find?

- Ⓐ $0.37
- Ⓑ $0.62
- Ⓒ $0.67
- Ⓓ $0.92

END OF PRACTICE SET

SOL Mathematics

Grade 3

Practice Test 3

Section 1

Instructions

Read each question carefully. For each multiple-choice question, fill in the circle for the correct answer. For other types of questions, follow the directions given in the question.

You may use a ruler to help you answer questions. You may not use a calculator on this test.

1   A bike ride was held to raise money. There were 70 riders and each rider paid $8 to enter. How much money was raised in all?

   Ⓐ $506
   Ⓑ $560
   Ⓒ $568
   Ⓓ $580

2   Sam read 39 pages of a novel in one week. He had 165 pages left to read. How many pages does the novel have? Write your answer below.

   _____

3   If the numbers below are each rounded to the nearest hundred, which **two** numbers will be rounded up?

   ☐   1,325
   ☐   5,682
   ☐   3,708
   ☐   1,935
   ☐   8,540
   ☐   2,854

4 Leonie has 20 books. She placed an equal number of books on 5 different shelves. There were no books left over.

Which number sentence shows how many books Leonie put on each shelf?

Ⓐ   20 + 5 = 25

Ⓑ   20 − 5 = 15

Ⓒ   20 × 5 = 100

Ⓓ   20 ÷ 5 = 4

5 Shade the stars below so that $\frac{1}{3}$ of the stars are shaded.

6 A square garden has side lengths of 8 inches. What is the area of the garden?

   Ⓐ   32 square inches

   Ⓑ   36 square inches

   Ⓒ   48 square inches

   Ⓓ   64 square inches

7 Look at the shaded figure below.

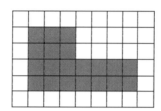

What is the area of the shaded figure?

   Ⓐ   20 square units

   Ⓑ   22 square units

   Ⓒ   26 square units

   Ⓓ   28 square units

8   Dannii is training for a bike race. She rode 17 miles on Monday, 19 miles on Tuesday, and 11 miles on Wednesday. Which is the best estimate of how far Dannii rode in all?

Ⓐ   30 miles

Ⓑ   40 miles

Ⓒ   50 miles

Ⓓ   60 miles

9   Squares and rectangles are quadrilaterals. Which of the shapes below is also a quadrilateral?

Ⓐ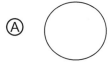

Ⓑ

Ⓒ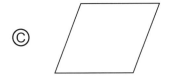

Ⓓ

10 The triangle below has a perimeter of 26 cm.

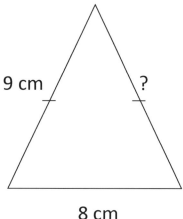

What is the length of the missing side? Write your answer below.

_____ cm

11 One Friday, 5 of a hairdresser's customers were male and 15 were female. What fraction of the hairdresser's customers were male? Write your answer below in lowest form. You can use the diagram below to help find your answer.

_____ of the customers

12 Which number comes next in the pattern below? Write your answer on the line below.

4, 8, 16, 32, 64, ____

13 Alana finished school at the time shown on the clock below.

Alana arrived home 15 minutes later. What time did Alana arrive home? Write your answer below.

_____ p.m.

14 A box contains 60 cans of soup. Gerald orders 8 boxes of soup for his store. How many cans of soup does Gerald order? Write your answer below.

_____ cans of soup

15 Lyn lives 15 miles from her school. Dan lives 3 miles closer than Lyn. How far does Dan live from school? Write your answer below.

_____ miles

16   The graph shows the number of points four players scored in a basketball game.

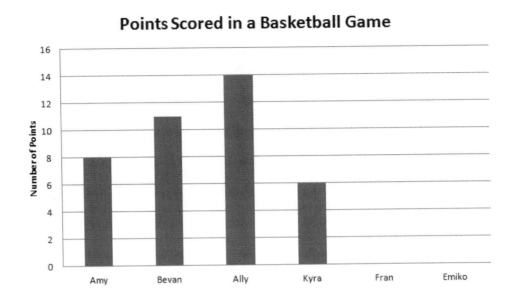

Fran scored 9 points and Emiko scored 5 points. Add two bars to the graph above to show the points scored by Fran and Emiko.

How many of the players scored more points than Fran? Write your answer below.

_____

17 Circle **all** the shapes below that are quadrilaterals.

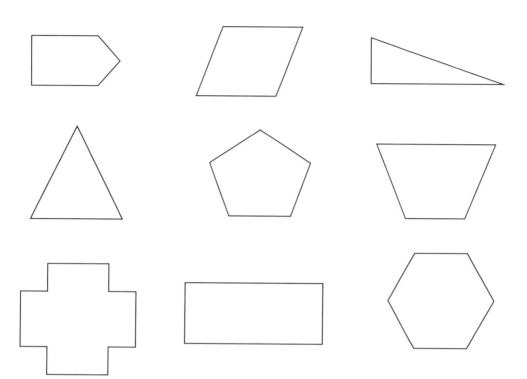

On the lines below, describe the property that is shared by all the shapes you circled.

_____

_____

_____

18 Look at the triangle below.

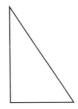

Circle **all** the shapes that appear to be congruent to the triangle.

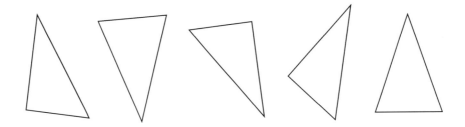

19 The top of a rectangular desk is 4 feet long and 3 feet wide. What is the area of the top of the desk? What is the perimeter of the top of the desk? Write your answers below.

Area: _____

Perimeter: _____

20 On the diagram below, what does the circled area of the diagram show?

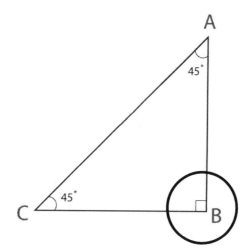

- Ⓐ A ray
- Ⓑ An angle
- Ⓒ A line segment
- Ⓓ A point

END OF PRACTICE SET

SOL Mathematics

Grade 3

Practice Test 3

Section 2

Instructions

Read each question carefully. For each multiple-choice question, fill in the circle for the correct answer. For other types of questions, follow the directions given in the question.

You may use a ruler to help you answer questions. You may not use a calculator on this test.

1   Mr. Porter is choosing dance partners for the girls in his class. He places the names of the boys in a hat. He then has each girl select a name from the hat.

Roland	Ewan	Davis
Greg	Colin	Archer

Emily selects first. What is the probability that Emily selects Colin?

Ⓐ   1 out of 5

Ⓑ   4 out of 5

Ⓒ   1 out of 6

Ⓓ   5 out of 6

2   The graph below shows the number of pets four girls have.

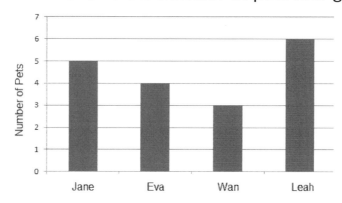

Which two girls have 10 pets in total? Write your answer below.

_____ and _____

3 Rory scored 28 points in a basketball game. Adam scored 4 points less than Rory. Danny scored 6 points more than Adam. How many points did Danny score?

- Ⓐ 18
- Ⓑ 30
- Ⓒ 26
- Ⓓ 38

4 Chan had a bag of 27 lollipops. He divided the lollipops evenly between several children.

If there were no lollipops left over, how many lollipops could each child have received? Complete the number sentences below to find the **two** possible answers.

☐ ÷ ☐ = ☐

☐ ÷ ☐ = ☐

5   Each square on the grid below is 1 cm wide and 1 cm high.

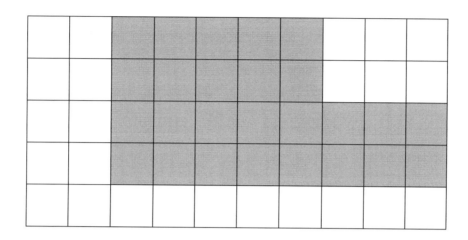

Which **two** expressions could be used to find the area of the shaded figure, in square centimeters?

☐   (5 x 4) + (3 x 2)

☐   (10 x 5) − (5 x 6)

☐   (8 x 2) + (5 x 4)

☐   (8 x 4) − (3 x 2)

☐   (8 x 4) − 3

☐   (10 x 5) − (2 x 6)

6 Look at the group of numbers below. Circle **all** the numbers that have an 8 in the tens place.

108	86	282
864	198	38

7 Joy is making gift cards. She puts stars on the front of each card. The table shows how many stars she uses for 3, 5, and 6 cards.

Number of Cards	Number of Stars
3	12
5	20
6	24
8	

Based on the table, how many stars would Joy need to make 8 cards?

Ⓐ 28
Ⓑ 32
Ⓒ 36
Ⓓ 26

8 Ling scored 82 on a reading test. Mickey scored 63 on the reading test. Which is the best estimate of how many more points Ling scored than Mickey?

- Ⓐ 10
- Ⓑ 15
- Ⓒ 20
- Ⓓ 25

9 The graph below shows the number of different types of trees in an orchard.

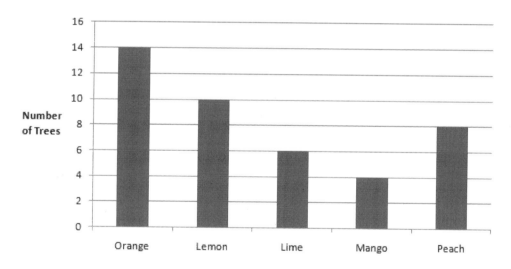

How many more orange trees are there than lime and mango trees combined? Write your answer below.

_____ trees

10 Mia bought a milkshake. She was given the change shown below. How much change was Mia given?

- Ⓐ $0.76
- Ⓑ $0.71
- Ⓒ $0.51
- Ⓓ $0.66

11 A rectangle has a length of 6 inches and a height of 5 inches. Complete the number sentences to show **two** ways to find the perimeter of the rectangle, in inches.

_____ + _____ + _____ + _____ = _____

2(_____ + _____) = _____

12 Gregory divided a rectangular piece of cardboard into sections, as shown below.

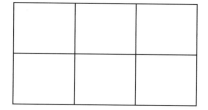

What fraction of the whole is each section?

Ⓐ $\frac{1}{2}$

Ⓑ $\frac{1}{3}$

Ⓒ $\frac{1}{5}$

Ⓓ $\frac{1}{6}$

13 What is the product of 9 and 8?

Ⓐ 56

Ⓑ 64

Ⓒ 72

Ⓓ 81

14 The grade 3 students at Sam's school are collecting cans for a food drive. The table below shows how many cans each class collected.

Class	Number of Cans
Miss Powell	39
Mr. Sato	22
Mrs. Joshi	26
Mr. Perez	37

Complete the list below by rounding each number to the nearest ten.

Miss Powell   40

Mr. Sato   20

Mrs. Joshi   30

Mr. Perez   40

15 Janine bought a packet of muffins. The packet contained 2 chocolate muffins and 6 vanilla muffins.

Complete the **two** fractions that show the fraction of muffins that are chocolate.

$$\frac{\boxed{}}{8} = \frac{\boxed{}}{4}$$

16 What fraction does point *J* represent?

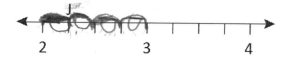

- Ⓐ $2\frac{1}{4}$
- Ⓑ $2\frac{1}{3}$
- Ⓒ $2\frac{1}{5}$
- Ⓓ $2\frac{1}{2}$

17 Which number sentence represents the array shown below?

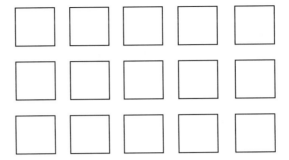

Ⓐ 5 + 3 = 8

Ⓑ 5 × 3 = 15

Ⓒ 15 × 3 = 45

Ⓓ 20 − 5 = 15

18 A pizza has 8 slices. Eriko wants to order enough pizza to have at least 62 slices. What is the least number of pizzas Eriko could order? Write your answer below.

_____ pizzas

19 Tina completes the calculation below.

$$8 \times 5 = 40$$

Write a division equation that Tina could use to check her calculation.

20 Troy swapped 2 quarters for coins with the same value. Which of these could Troy have swapped his 2 quarters for?

- Ⓐ 25 pennies
- Ⓑ 20 nickels
- Ⓒ 10 nickels
- Ⓓ 10 dimes

END OF PRACTICE SET

SOL Mathematics

Grade 3

Practice Test 4

Section 1

Instructions

Read each question carefully. For each multiple-choice question, fill in the circle for the correct answer. For other types of questions, follow the directions given in the question.

You may use a ruler to help you answer questions. You may not use a calculator on this test.

1   Habib measured the length of each wall of his room. A diagram of Habib's room is shown below.

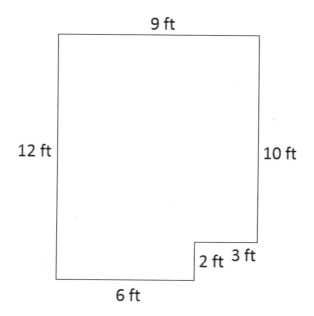

What is the perimeter of Habib's room?
- Ⓐ 37 ft
- Ⓑ 40 ft
- Ⓒ 39 ft
- Ⓓ 42 ft

2   Apples are sold in bags. There are the same number of apples in each bag. The table below shows the number of apples in 2, 3, and 4 bags. Complete the table to show the number of apples in 6 bags.

Number of Bags	Number of Apples
2	12
3	18
4	24
6	

3   Which of the following shapes is a pentagon?

Ⓐ

Ⓑ

Ⓒ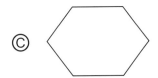

Ⓓ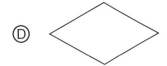

4   Toni has tokens for arcade games.

If Toni counts her tokens in groups of 6, which list shows only numbers she would count?

Ⓐ   6, 8, 10, 12

Ⓑ   6, 10, 16, 20

Ⓒ   12, 18, 24, 30

Ⓓ   12, 16, 20, 24

5   Sarah, Marco, and Devon each ate $\frac{1}{8}$ of a pizza. Which of these is equal to $\frac{1}{8} + \frac{1}{8} + \frac{1}{8}$ and tells how much pizza they ate in all?

Ⓐ $\frac{3}{8}$

Ⓑ $\frac{1}{512}$

Ⓒ $\frac{1}{24}$

Ⓓ $\frac{3}{24}$

6   There are 36 students in a class. The teacher needs to divide the students in the class into teams. Each team must have the same number of students in it. There cannot be any students left over. Which of the following could describe the teams? Select **all** the correct answers.

☐   7 teams of 4 students

☐   9 teams of 4 students

☐   6 teams of 5 students

☐   6 teams of 6 students

☐   8 teams of 4 students

☐   9 teams of 3 students

7   The pictograph shows the emails Sammy sent each week day.

Monday	✉✉✉
Tuesday	✉✉
Wednesday	✉✉✉✉
Thursday	✉✉✉
Friday	✉✉✉✉✉

Each ✉ means 2 emails.

How many emails did Sammy send on Wednesday? Write your answer below.

_____ emails

8   What time is shown on the clock below?

- Ⓐ   6:30
- Ⓑ   7:30
- Ⓒ   6:15
- Ⓓ   6:45

9   A square garden has side lengths of 8 inches. Jackie makes a rectangular garden with the same area as the square garden. Which of these could be the dimensions of the rectangular garden?

- Ⓐ   10 inches by 6 inches
- Ⓑ   7 inches by 9 inches
- Ⓒ   8 inches by 12 inches
- Ⓓ   16 inches by 4 inches

10 Naomi is making a pictograph to show how many fruit trees there are in her yard. The pictograph she has made so far is shown below.

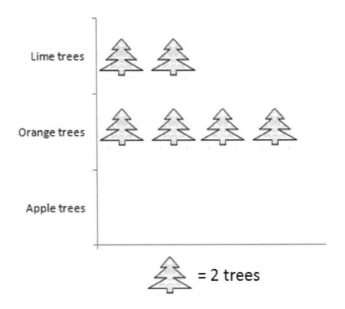

There are 6 apple trees in Naomi's yard. How many tree symbols should Naomi use to show 6 apple trees?

Ⓐ 3

Ⓑ 2

Ⓒ 12

Ⓓ 6

11 Which measurement is the most likely length of a crayon?

    Ⓐ 4 feet

    Ⓑ 4 inches

    Ⓒ 4 yards

    Ⓓ 4 miles

12 Shade the model below to show a fraction equivalent to $\frac{1}{4}$.

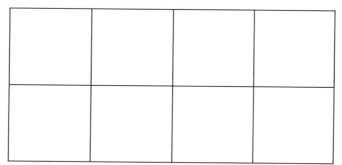

13 A school has 4 school buses. Each bus can seat 48 students. What is the total number of students the buses can seat? Write your answer below.

_____ students

14 What is the length of the piece of lace shown below?

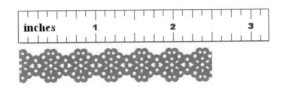

Ⓐ 2 inches

Ⓑ $2\frac{1}{2}$ inches

Ⓒ $2\frac{1}{3}$ inches

Ⓓ $2\frac{1}{4}$ inches

15 Ribbon costs $4 per yard. Allie has $24 to spend on ribbon. Which equation could be used to find how many yards of ribbon, *y*, she can buy?

Ⓐ 4 × 24 = y

Ⓑ 4 ÷ 24 = y

Ⓒ 4 × y = 24

Ⓓ 4 ÷ y = 24

16 Reggie's train leaves at the time shown on the clock below.

What time does Reggie's train leave?

- Ⓐ 3:00
- Ⓑ 1:15
- Ⓒ 1:10
- Ⓓ 3:05

17 What do the shaded models below show?

- Ⓐ $\frac{5}{12} > \frac{1}{3}$
- Ⓑ $\frac{5}{12} = \frac{1}{3}$
- Ⓒ $\frac{5}{12} < \frac{4}{12}$
- Ⓓ $\frac{5}{7} < \frac{2}{3}$

18. Which number sentence represents the array shown below?

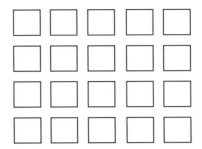

Ⓐ 5 + 4 = 9

Ⓑ 5 × 5 = 25

Ⓒ 5 × 4 = 20

Ⓓ 5 − 4 = 1

19. Lydia eats 2 pieces of fruit every day. Complete the table to show how many pieces of fruit Lydia eats in 5, 7, and 14 days.

Number of Days	Number of Pieces of Fruit
5	
7	
14	

20 Melinda buys bagels in packets of 4.

If Melinda counts the bagels in groups of 4, which numbers would she count? Circle **all** the numbers she would count.

18	20	22	26
30	32	42	44

END OF PRACTICE SET

SOL Mathematics

Grade 3

Practice Test 4

Section 2

Instructions

Read each question carefully. For each multiple-choice question, fill in the circle for the correct answer. For other types of questions, follow the directions given in the question.

You may use a ruler to help you answer questions. You may not use a calculator on this test.

1   Tim scored 21 points in a basketball game. Emmett scored 7 more points than Tim. Which method can be used to find how many points Tim and Emmett scored together?

   Ⓐ   Add 21 and 7
   Ⓑ   Add 21 to the sum of 21 and 7
   Ⓒ   Add 21 to the difference of 21 and 7
   Ⓓ   Subtract 7 from 21

2   Place the fractions below in order from smallest to greatest. You can use the fraction bars to help you order the fractions.

   Write the numbers 1, 2, 3, and 4 on the lines to show the order.

   ____ $\frac{7}{10}$ ____ $\frac{4}{5}$ ____ $\frac{1}{5}$ ____ $\frac{9}{10}$

3 There are 28 students at basketball training. The coach needs to divide the students into groups. Each group must have the same number of students in it. There cannot be any students left over. Which of the following could describe the groups?

   Ⓐ 7 groups of 4 students

   Ⓑ 8 groups of 3 students

   Ⓒ 6 groups of 4 students

   Ⓓ 10 groups of 3 students

4 Annie collects baseball cards. She has 22 cards in her collection. She gave her sister 2 baseball cards. Then Annie bought 4 new baseball cards. Which expression can be used to find the number of baseball cards Annie has now?

   Ⓐ 22 + 2 + 4

   Ⓑ 22 + 2 − 4

   Ⓒ 22 − 2 + 4

   Ⓓ 22 − 2 − 4

5   Nate plotted a fraction on the number line below.

Which fractions could Nate have been plotting? Select **all** the correct answers.

☐ $\frac{1}{2}$

☐ $\frac{2}{2}$

☐ $\frac{4}{2}$

☐ $\frac{8}{4}$

☐ $\frac{4}{8}$

6   The pictograph below shows how long Tamika spent at the computer each week day.

Monday	🖥🖥🖥🖥
Tuesday	🖥🖥🖥🖥🖥🖥
Wednesday	🖥🖥🖥🖥🖥
Thursday	🖥🖥🖥
Friday	🖥🖥

Each 🖥 means 10 minutes.

How long did Tamika spend at the computer on Wednesday?

Ⓐ   15 minutes

Ⓑ   60 minutes

Ⓒ   5 minutes

Ⓓ   50 minutes

7   A recipe for meatballs calls for $\frac{1}{2}$ teaspoon of cumin. Complete the fractions below to show **two** fractions equivalent to $\frac{1}{2}$.

$$\frac{\square}{6} \quad \text{and} \quad \frac{6}{\square}$$

8 Dean drew these shapes.

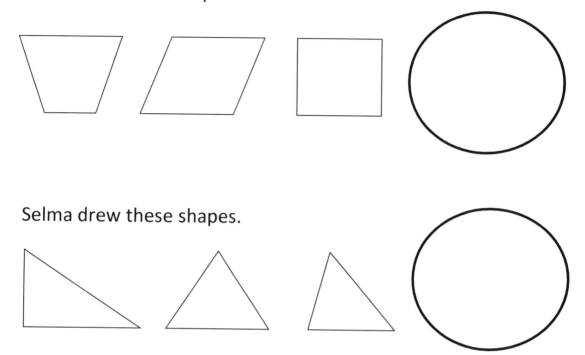

Selma drew these shapes.

Add **one** of the shapes below that fits with Dean's shapes and **one** of the shapes below that fits with Selma's shapes. Draw each shape in the empty circle.

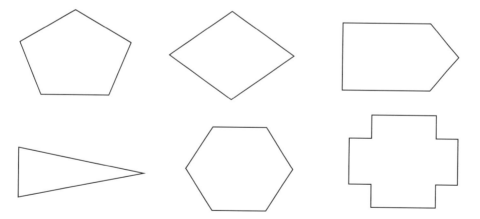

9 A piece of square note paper has side lengths of 5 inches each. What is the perimeter of the note paper?

- Ⓐ 10 inches
- Ⓑ 20 inches
- Ⓒ 25 inches
- Ⓓ 30 inches

10 The table below shows the colors of blocks in a bag.

Color	Number of Blocks
Red	6
Green	4
Blue	7
White	2

If Andre picks one block at random, which color will he be least likely to pick?

- Ⓐ Red
- Ⓑ Green
- Ⓒ Blue
- Ⓓ White

11 Plot the number 48 on the number line below.

What is the number 48 rounded to the nearest ten? Write your answer below.

_____

On the lines below, explain how the number line helped you round the number.

_____

_____

_____

_____

_____

12 Apple trees were planted in rows. Each row had the same number of apple trees. Complete the missing numbers in the table below.

Number of Rows	Number of Apple Trees
4	24
5	30
6	36
7	42
8	
9	
10	

13 Mrs. Anderson took out a loan that will take her 60 months to pay off. How many years will it take Mrs. Anderson to pay off the loan? Write your answer below.

1 year = 12 months

_____ years

14 Georgia shaded the shape below.

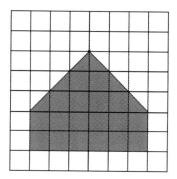

Each square on the grid measures 1 square centimeter. What is the area of the shaded shape? Write your answer below.

_____ square centimeters

15 The table below shows how many customers a restaurant had on each day of the week.

Day	Number of Customers
Monday	28
Tuesday	21
Wednesday	36
Thursday	32
Friday	45

How many more customers did the restaurant have on Friday than on Monday? Write your answer below.

_____ customers

16 The table below shows Emma's savings over four months.

Month	Amount Saved ($)
Jan	18
Feb	16
Mar	14
Apr	19

Complete the graph below using the data in the table.

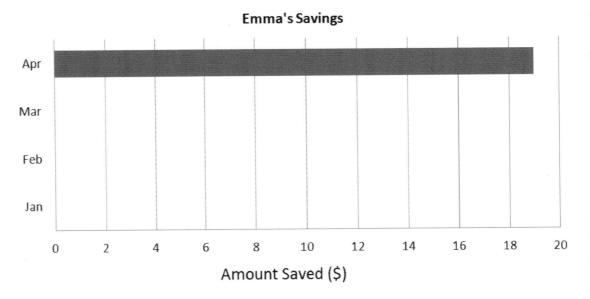

What is the difference between the most and the least she saved each month? Write your answer below.

$ _____

17 Look at the number pattern below.

$$7, 10, 13, 16, 19, 22, \underline{}$$

If the pattern continues, which number will come next? Write your answer below.

_____

On the lines below, explain how you found your answer.

_____

_____

_____

_____

18. Kai found the coins shown below in the sofa. What is the value of the coins that Kai found?

Ⓐ $1.26

Ⓑ $1.36

Ⓒ $1.45

Ⓓ $2.36

19 During a golf game, Gia scored below par on 3 of the 18 holes.

Divide the rectangle below into segments and shade the rectangle to show what fraction of the holes Gia scored below par on.

What fraction of the holes did Gia score below par on? Write your answer below in lowest form.

_____

20 What are the two smallest 3-digit numbers that can be made using the digits 1, 6, and 4? Each digit must be used only once in each number. Write the two numbers below.

_____ and _____

On the lines below, explain how you found your answer.

_____

_____

_____

_____

END OF PRACTICE SET

ANSWER KEY

Virginia's New State Standards

In 2016, the state of Virginia adopted new *Standards of Learning*. The *Standards of Learning* describe what students are expected to know. Student learning throughout the year is based on these standards, and all the questions on the SOL Mathematics assessments cover these standards. All the exercises and questions in this book cover the *Standards of Learning* introduced in 2016.

Assessing Skills and Knowledge

The skills listed in the *Standards of Learning* are divided into five topics. These are:

- Number and Number Sense
- Computation and Estimation
- Measurement and Geometry
- Probability and Statistics
- Patterns, Functions, and Algebra

The answer key identifies the topic for each question. Use the topics listed to identify general areas of strength and weakness. Then target revision and instruction accordingly.

The answer key also identifies the specific math skill that each question is testing. Use the skills listed to identify skills that the student is lacking. Then target revision and instruction accordingly.

Scoring Questions

This book includes questions where a task needs to be completed or a written answer is provided. The answer key gives guidance on what to look for in the answer and how to score these questions. Use the criteria listed as a guide to scoring these questions, and as a guide for giving the student advice on how to improve an answer.

SOL Mathematics, Mini-Test 1

Question	Answer	Topic	Mathematics Standard
1	B	Number and Number Sense	Name and write fractions and mixed numbers represented by a model.
2	B	Measurement and Geometry	Solve practical problems related to elapsed time in one-hour increments within a 12-hour period.
3	A	Measurement and Geometry	Estimate and measure liquid volume in cups, pints, quarts, gallons, and liters.
4	triangle pentagon hexagon octagon	Measurement and Geometry	Identify and name polygons with 10 or fewer sides.
5	1st, 3rd, 5th, and 6th	Computation and Estimation	Represent multiplication and division through 10 × 10, using a variety of approaches and models.
6	See Below	Number and Number Sense	Represent fractions and mixed numbers with models and symbols.
7	See Below	Probability and Statistics	Collect, organize, and represent data in pictographs or bar graphs.
8	See Below	Measurement and Geometry	Identify and name polygons with 10 or fewer sides.
9	See Below	Measurement and Geometry	Estimate and count the number of square units needed to cover a given surface in order to determine its area. Estimate and measure the distance around a polygon in order to determine its perimeter using U.S. customary and metric units.
10	B	Probability and Statistics	Read and interpret data represented in pictographs and bar graphs.

Q6.
The numbers should be plotted as below.

Scoring Information
Give a total score out of 2.
Give a score of 0.5 for each number correctly plotted.

Q7.
The graph should be completed with a bar to 12 for Action, a bar to 14 for Comedy, and a bar to 8 for Drama.

Scoring Information
Give a total score out of 3.
Give a score of 1 for each bar correctly added.

Q8.
The student should circle the pentagon.
The student should explain that the shape has 5 sides instead of 3 sides. The student may identify that the shape is a pentagon.

Scoring Information
Give a total score out of 3.
Give a score of 1 for circling the pentagon.
Give a score out of 2 for the explanation.

Q9.
The student should complete the missing dimensions of 2 ft and 11 ft.
The student may divide the shape into a 3 by 7 rectangle and a 2 by 8 rectangle or a 3 by 5 rectangle and an 11 by 2 rectangle.
The student should find an area of 37 square feet.
The student should find a perimeter of 36 feet.

Scoring Information
Give a total score out of 4.
Give a score of 0.5 for each correct missing dimension.
Give a score of 1 for dividing the shape correctly.
Give a score of 1 for the correct area.
Give a score of 1 for the correct perimeter.

SOL Mathematics, Mini-Test 2

Question	Answer	Topic	Mathematics Standard
1	C	Computation and Estimation	Create and solve single-step and multistep practical problems involving sums or differences of two whole numbers, each 9,999 or less.
2	5, 10, 15, 20, 25	Patterns, Functions, and Algebra	Identify, describe, create, and extend patterns found in objects, pictures, numbers and tables.
3	B	Measurement and Geometry	Tell time to the nearest minute, using analog and digital clocks.
4	1st and 4th	Measurement and Geometry	Identify and describe congruent and noncongruent figures.
5	2nd, 3rd, and 4th	Number and Number Sense	Compare fractions having like and unlike denominators, using words and symbols (>, <, =, or ≠), with models.
6	C	Computation and Estimation	Create and solve single-step practical problems that involve multiplication and division through 10 x 10.
7	$717	Computation and Estimation	Create and solve single-step and multistep practical problems involving sums or differences of two whole numbers, each 9,999 or less.
8	See Below	Patterns, Functions, and Algebra	Identify, describe, create, and extend patterns found in objects, pictures, numbers and tables.
9	See Below	Probability and Statistics	Read and interpret data represented in pictographs and bar graphs.
10	See Below	Measurement and Geometry	Estimate and count the number of square units needed to cover a given surface in order to determine its area.

Q8.
26, 30, 34, 38
The student should identify that all the numbers will be even. The student should explain that all the numbers will be even because an even number is always being added to an even number.

Scoring Information
Give a total score out of 4.
Give a score of 0.5 for each correct number in the pattern.
Give a score of 1 for identifying that all the numbers will be even and a score out of 1 for the explanation.

Q9.
Friday
40 minutes
30 minutes

Scoring Information
Give a total score out of 3.
Give a score of 1 for each correct answer.

Q10.
Rectangle 1: 2 by 4 units   Rectangle 2: 2 by 6 units
Area: 20 square units

Scoring Information
Give a total score out of 3.
Give a score of 1 for each correct answer.

SOL Mathematics, Practice Test 1, Section 1

Question	Answer	Topic	Mathematics Standard
1	18, 30, 36, 42	Computation and Estimation	Create and solve single-step practical problems that involve multiplication and division through 10 x 10.
2	Wednesday	Probability and Statistics	Read and interpret data represented in pictographs and bar graphs.
3	$\frac{4}{1}$ and $\frac{12}{3}$	Number and Number Sense	Compare fractions having like and unlike denominators, using words and symbols (>, <, =, or ≠), with models.
4	B	Probability and Statistics	Collect, organize, and represent data in pictographs or bar graphs.
5	B	Computation and Estimation	Create and solve single-step practical problems that involve multiplication and division through 10 x 10.
6	C	Patterns, Functions, and Algebra	Create equations to represent equivalent mathematical relationships.
7	5,600	Number and Number Sense	Round whole numbers, 9,999 or less, to the nearest ten, hundred, and thousand.
8	1,500 + 1,600 + 1,200 = 4,300	Number and Number Sense	Round whole numbers, 9,999 or less, to the nearest ten, hundred, and thousand.
9	A	Computation and Estimation	Create and solve single-step and multistep practical problems involving sums or differences of two whole numbers, each 9,999 or less.
10	Point at $1\frac{1}{4}$	Number and Number Sense	Represent fractions and mixed numbers with models and symbols.
11	See Below	Number and Number Sense	Round whole numbers, 9,999 or less, to the nearest ten, hundred, and thousand.
12	$\frac{5}{19}$	Number and Number Sense	Name and write fractions and mixed numbers represented by a model.
13	See Below	Number and Number Sense	Compare fractions having like and unlike denominators, using words and symbols (>, <, =, or ≠), with models.
14	See Below	Patterns, Functions, and Algebra	Identify, describe, create, and extend patterns found in objects, pictures, numbers and tables.
15	35°C	Measurement and Geometry	Read temperature to the nearest degree.
16	C	Computation and Estimation	Solve single-step practical problems involving multiplication of whole numbers, where one factor is 99 or less and the second factor is 5 or less.
17	30 – 6 + 2 = 26	Computation and Estimation	Create and solve single-step and multistep practical problems involving sums or differences of two whole numbers, each 9,999 or less.
18	A	Number and Number Sense	Read, write, and identify the place and value of each digit in a six-digit whole number, with and without models.
19	D	Number and Number Sense	Name and write fractions and mixed numbers represented by a model.
20	D	Measurement and Geometry	Identify equivalent periods of time and solve practical problems related to equivalent periods of time.

Q11.
110, 90, 280, 980, 860, 200, 40, 770

The student should provide an explanation that refers to considering the number in the ones place. The answer should include that the number is rounded down if the number is less than 5 and rounded up if the number is 5 or higher.

Scoring Information
Give a total score out of 4.
Give a score of 0.25 for each number correctly rounded.
Give a score out of 2 for the explanation.

Q13.
The two models should have shaded 3 of the 10 segments and 2 of the 10 segments.
The > symbol should be placed in the empty box.

The student may explain how shading the models allows the two fractions to be compared by seeing how many parts of 10 each fraction is. The student may explain how you can compare the fractions as parts of the same whole.

Scoring Information
Give a total score out of 4.
Give a score of 1 for each correct shading.
Give a score of 1 for the correct symbol.
Give a score out of 2 for the explanation.

Q14.
Expression: $x + 3$
Answer: 34
Answer: 115

Scoring Information
Give a total score out of 3.
Give a score of 1 for the correct expression.
Give a score of 1 for each correct answer.

SOL Mathematics, Practice Test 1, Section 2

Question	Answer	Topic	Mathematics Standard
1	A	Measurement and Geometry	Identify and describe congruent and noncongruent figures.
2	A	Computation and Estimation	Create and solve single-step practical problems that involve multiplication and division through 10 x 10.
3	B	Measurement and Geometry	Estimate and count the number of square units needed to cover a given surface in order to determine its area.
4	B	Measurement and Geometry	Identify equivalent periods of time and solve practical problems related to equivalent periods of time.
5	D	Measurement and Geometry	Estimate and measure length to the nearest $\frac{1}{2}$ inch, inch, foot, yard, centimeter, and meter.
6	D	Patterns, Functions, and Algebra	Identify, describe, create, and extend patterns found in objects, pictures, numbers and tables.
7	16 cans	Probability and Statistics	Read and interpret data represented in pictographs and bar graphs.
8	C	Measurement and Geometry	Estimate and measure the distance around a polygon in order to determine its perimeter using U.S. customary and metric units.
9	75, 90, 105	Patterns, Functions, and Algebra	Identify, describe, create, and extend patterns found in objects, pictures, numbers and tables.
10	14°	Measurement and Geometry	Read temperature to the nearest degree.
11	See Below	Number and Number Sense	Round whole numbers, 9,999 or less, to the nearest ten, hundred, and thousand.
12	$6	Computation and Estimation	Create and solve single-step practical problems that involve multiplication and division through 10 x 10.
13	180 minutes	Measurement and Geometry	Solve practical problems related to elapsed time in one-hour increments within a 12-hour period. Identify equivalent periods of time and solve practical problems related to equivalent periods of time.
14	See Below	Number and Number Sense	Compare fractions having like and unlike denominators, using words and symbols (>, <, =, or ≠), with models.
15	See Below	Measurement and Geometry	Estimate and measure the distance around a polygon in order to determine its perimeter using U.S. customary and metric units. Estimate and count the number of square units needed to cover a given surface in order to determine its area.
16	B	Probability and Statistics	Collect, organize, and represent data in pictographs or bar graphs.
17	D	Computation and Estimation	Create and solve single-step and multistep practical problems involving sums or differences of two whole numbers, each 9,999 or less.
18	$575	Computation and Estimation	Create and solve single-step and multistep practical problems involving sums or differences of two whole numbers, each 9,999 or less.
19	B	Computation and Estimation	Create and solve single-step practical problems that involve multiplication and division through 10 x 10.
20	A	Measurement and Geometry	Estimate and measure the distance around a polygon in order to determine its perimeter using U.S. customary and metric units.

Q11.
Nearest ten: 8,780
Nearest hundred: 8,800

The student should provide an explanation that refers to considering the number in the ones place when rounding to the nearest ten and considering the number in the tens place when rounding to the nearest hundred. The answer should include that the number is rounded down if the number is less than 5 and rounded up if the number is 5 or higher.

Scoring Information
Give a total score out of 4.
Give a score of 1 for each correct rounding.
Give a score out of 2 for the explanation.

Q14.
The halves fraction bar should have 1 of the 2 segments shaded.
The quarters fraction bar should have 2 of the 4 segments shaded.
The eighths fraction bar should have 4 of the 8 segments shaded.
Fraction: $\frac{4}{8}$

Scoring Information
Give a total score out of 4.
Give a score of 1 for each fraction bar correctly shaded.
Give a score of 1 for the correct fraction.

Q15.
18 square units
The grid should have a 6 by 3 rectangle drawn on it.

Scoring Information
Give a total score out of 3.
Give a score of 1 for the correct area.
Give a score of 2 for a 6 by 3 rectangle.
Give a score of 1 for a non-rectangular shape with an area of 18 square units.

SOL Mathematics, Practice Test 2, Section 1

Question	Answer	Topic	Mathematics Standard
1	C	Measurement and Geometry	Estimate and measure the distance around a polygon in order to determine its perimeter using U.S. customary and metric units.
2	D	Measurement and Geometry	Estimate and count the number of square units needed to cover a given surface in order to determine its area.
3	3rd and 4th	Computation and Estimation	Create and solve single-step and multistep practical problems involving sums or differences of two whole numbers, each 9,999 or less.
4	1,300 1,290	Number and Number Sense	Round whole numbers, 9,999 or less, to the nearest ten, hundred, and thousand.
5	C	Computation and Estimation	Represent multiplication and division through 10 × 10, using a variety of approaches and models.
6	C	Measurement and Geometry	Make change from $5.00 or less.
7	A	Measurement and Geometry	Estimate and count the number of square units needed to cover a given surface in order to determine its area.
8	C	Computation and Estimation	Estimate and determine the sum or difference of two whole numbers.
9	C	Computation and Estimation	Represent multiplication and division through 10 × 10, using a variety of approaches and models.
10	1, 0	Computation and Estimation	Demonstrate fluency with multiplication facts of 0, 1, 2, 5, and 10.
11	4 miles Ryan and Leah 6 miles	Probability and Statistics	Read and interpret data represented in pictographs and bar graphs.
12	B	Measurement and Geometry	Estimate and count the number of square units needed to cover a given surface in order to determine its area.
13	B	Computation and Estimation	Estimate and determine the sum or difference of two whole numbers.
14	$\frac{2}{6}$ and $\frac{1}{3}$	Number and Number Sense	Compare fractions having like and unlike denominators, using words and symbols (>, <, =, or ≠), with models.
15	C	Computation and Estimation	Represent multiplication and division through 10 × 10, using a variety of approaches and models.
16	Point at $2\frac{3}{4}$	Number and Number Sense	Represent fractions and mixed numbers with models and symbols.
17	Red $\frac{1}{4}$ Green $\frac{1}{2}$ Blue $\frac{1}{10}$ White $\frac{3}{20}$	Probability and Statistics	Investigate and describe the concept of probability as a measurement of chance and list possible outcomes for a single event.
18	24 pieces of pie	Computation and Estimation	Create and solve single-step practical problems that involve multiplication and division through 10 x 10.
19	$\frac{1}{8}, \frac{1}{4}, \frac{3}{10}$	Number and Number Sense	Compare fractions having like and unlike denominators, using words and symbols (>, <, =, or ≠), with models.
20	150 + 150 + 50 + 50 = 400 2(150 + 50) = 400	Measurement and Geometry	Estimate and measure the distance around a polygon in order to determine its perimeter using U.S. customary and metric units.

SOL Mathematics, Practice Test 2, Section 2

Question	Answer	Topic	Mathematics Standard
1	A	Measurement and Geometry	Combine and subdivide polygons with three or four sides and name the resulting polygon(s).
2	D	Number and Number Sense	Read, write, and identify the place and value of each digit in a six-digit whole number, with and without models.
3	$3 50 muffins	Patterns, Functions, and Algebra	Identify, describe, create, and extend patterns found in objects, pictures, numbers and tables.
4	36 cm²	Measurement and Geometry	Estimate and count the number of square units needed to cover a given surface in order to determine its area.
5	A	Computation and Estimation	Solve single-step practical problems involving multiplication of whole numbers, where one factor is 99 or less and the second factor is 5 or less.
6	B	Number and Number Sense	Compare and order whole numbers, each 9,999 or less.
7	Tuesday 13° 9°	Probability and Statistics	Read and interpret data represented in pictographs and bar graphs.
8	Any 3 of the 4 squares shaded, $\frac{3}{4}$	Number and Number Sense	Compare fractions having like and unlike denominators, using words and symbols (>, <, =, or ≠), with models.
9	1st and 6th	Computation and Estimation	Create and solve single-step practical problems that involve multiplication and division through 10 x 10.
10	D	Computation and Estimation	Create and solve single-step and multistep practical problems involving sums or differences of two whole numbers, each 9,999 or less.
11	B	Probability and Statistics	Read and interpret data represented in pictographs and bar graphs.
12	B	Probability and Statistics	Collect, organize, and represent data in pictographs or bar graphs.
13	16, 32, 40	Patterns, Functions, and Algebra	Identify, describe, create, and extend patterns found in objects, pictures, numbers and tables.
14	24, 28	Patterns, Functions, and Algebra	Identify, describe, create, and extend patterns found in objects, pictures, numbers and tables.
15	A	Number and Number Sense	Name and write fractions and mixed numbers represented by a model.
16	A	Number and Number Sense	Represent fractions and mixed numbers with models and symbols.
17	$\frac{2}{5}$	Number and Number Sense	Represent fractions and mixed numbers with models and symbols.
18	C	Measurement and Geometry	Estimate and measure liquid volume in cups, pints, quarts, gallons, and liters.
19	C	Computation and Estimation	Create and solve single-step and multistep practical problems involving sums or differences of two whole numbers, each 9,999 or less.
20	B	Measurement and Geometry	Determine the value of a collection of bills and coins whose total value is $5.00 or less.

SOL Mathematics, Practice Test 3, Section 1

Question	Answer	Topic	Mathematics Standard
1	B	Computation and Estimation	Demonstrate fluency with multiplication facts of 0, 1, 2, 5, and 10.
2	204	Computation and Estimation	Estimate and determine the sum or difference of two whole numbers.
3	5,682 2,854	Number and Number Sense	Round whole numbers, 9,999 or less, to the nearest ten, hundred, and thousand.
4	D	Computation and Estimation	Represent multiplication and division through 10 × 10, using a variety of approaches and models.
5	Any 3 of the 9 stars shaded	Number and Number Sense	Represent fractions and mixed numbers with models and symbols.
6	D	Measurement and Geometry	Estimate and count the number of square units needed to cover a given surface in order to determine its area.
7	A	Measurement and Geometry	Estimate and count the number of square units needed to cover a given surface in order to determine its area.
8	C	Computation and Estimation	Estimate and determine the sum or difference of two whole numbers.
9	C	Measurement and Geometry	Identify and name polygons with 10 or fewer sides.
10	9 cm	Measurement and Geometry	Estimate and measure the distance around a polygon in order to determine its perimeter using U.S. customary and metric units.
11	$\frac{1}{4}$ of the customers	Number and Number Sense	Name and write fractions and mixed numbers represented by a model.
12	128	Patterns, Functions, and Algebra	Identify, describe, create, and extend patterns found in objects, pictures, numbers and tables.
13	3:45 p.m.	Measurement and Geometry	Tell time to the nearest minute, using analog and digital clocks.
14	480	Computation and Estimation	Demonstrate fluency with multiplication facts of 0, 1, 2, 5, and 10.
15	12 miles	Computation and Estimation	Create and solve single-step and multistep practical problems involving sums or differences of two whole numbers, each 9,999 or less.
16	Bar to 9 Bar to 5 2 players	Probability and Statistics	Collect, organize, and represent data in pictographs or bar graphs. Read and interpret data represented in pictographs and bar graphs.
17	See Below	Measurement and Geometry	Identify and name polygons with 10 or fewer sides.
18	1st, 3rd, 4th	Measurement and Geometry	Identify and describe congruent and noncongruent figures.
19	12 square feet 14 feet	Measurement and Geometry	Estimate and measure the distance around a polygon in order to determine its perimeter using U.S. customary and metric units. Estimate and count the number of square units needed to cover a given surface in order to determine its area.
20	B	Measurement and Geometry	Identify and draw representations of points, lines, line segments, rays, and angles.

Q17.
The rhombus, the trapezoid, and the rectangle should be circled.
The property identified could be that all the shapes have four sides or that all the shapes have four angles.

Scoring Information
Give a total score out of 4.
Give a score of 1 for each shape correctly circled. Take off 1 point for each additional shape incorrectly circled.
Give a score out of 1 for the explanation.

SOL Mathematics, Practice Test 3, Section 2

Question	Answer	Topic	Mathematics Standard
1	C	Probability and Statistics	Investigate and describe the concept of probability as a measurement of chance and list possible outcomes for a single event.
2	Eva, Leah	Probability and Statistics	Read and interpret data represented in pictographs and bar graphs.
3	B	Computation and Estimation	Represent multiplication and division through 10 × 10, using a variety of approaches and models.
4	27 ÷ 3 = 9 27 ÷ 9 = 3	Computation and Estimation	Create and solve single-step practical problems that involve multiplication and division through 10 x 10.
5	1st and 4th	Measurement and Geometry	Estimate and count the number of square units needed to cover a given surface in order to determine its area.
6	86, 282	Number and Number Sense	Read, write, and identify the place and value of each digit in a six-digit whole number, with and without models.
7	B	Patterns, Functions, and Algebra	Identify, describe, create, and extend patterns found in objects, pictures, numbers and tables.
8	C	Computation and Estimation	Estimate and determine the sum or difference of two whole numbers.
9	4 trees	Measurement and Geometry	Read and interpret data represented in pictographs and bar graphs.
10	A	Measurement and Geometry	Determine the value of a collection of bills and coins whose total value is $5.00 or less.
11	6 + 5 + 6 + 5 = 22 2(6 + 5) = 22	Measurement and Geometry	Estimate and measure the distance around a polygon in order to determine its perimeter using U.S. customary and metric units.
12	D	Number and Number Sense	Name and write fractions and mixed numbers represented by a model.
13	C	Computation and Estimation	Create and solve single-step practical problems that involve multiplication and division through 10 x 10.
14	20, 30, 40	Number and Number Sense	Round whole numbers, 9,999 or less, to the nearest ten, hundred, and thousand.
15	$\frac{2}{8} = \frac{1}{4}$	Number and Number Sense	Compare fractions having like and unlike denominators, using words and symbols (>, <, =, or ≠), with models.
16	A	Number and Number Sense	Name and write fractions and mixed numbers represented by a model.
17	B	Computation and Estimation	Represent multiplication and division through 10 × 10, using a variety of approaches and models.
18	8 pizzas	Computation and Estimation	Create and solve single-step practical problems that involve multiplication and division through 10 x 10.
19	40 ÷ 8 = 5 or 40 ÷ 5 = 8	Computation and Estimation	Represent multiplication and division through 10 × 10, using a variety of approaches and models.
20	C	Measurement and Geometry	Compare the value of two sets of coins or two sets of coins and bills.

SOL Mathematics, Practice Test 4, Section 1

Question	Answer	Topic	Mathematics Standard
1	D	Measurement and Geometry	Estimate and measure the distance around a polygon in order to determine its perimeter using U.S. customary and metric units.
2	36	Patterns, Functions, and Algebra	Identify, describe, create, and extend patterns found in objects, pictures, numbers and tables.
3	A	Measurement and Geometry	Identify and name polygons with 10 or fewer sides.
4	C	Computation and Estimation	Create and solve single-step practical problems that involve multiplication and division through 10 x 10.
5	A	Computation and Estimation	Solve practical problems that involve addition and subtraction with proper fractions having like denominators of 12 or less.
6	2nd and 4th	Computation and Estimation	Create and solve single-step practical problems that involve multiplication and division through 10 x 10.
7	8 emails	Probability and Statistics	Read and interpret data represented in pictographs and bar graphs.
8	B	Measurement and Geometry	Tell time to the nearest minute, using analog and digital clocks.
9	D	Measurement and Geometry	Estimate and count the number of square units needed to cover a given surface in order to determine its area.
10	A	Probability and Statistics	Collect, organize, and represent data in pictographs or bar graphs.
11	B	Measurement and Geometry	Estimate and measure length to the nearest $\frac{1}{2}$ inch, inch, foot, yard, centimeter, and meter.
12	Any 2 of the 8 squares shaded	Number and Number Sense	Compare fractions having like and unlike denominators, using words and symbols (>, <, =, or ≠), with models.
13	192 students	Computation and Estimation	Solve single-step practical problems involving multiplication of whole numbers, where one factor is 99 or less and the second factor is 5 or less.
14	B	Measurement and Geometry	Estimate and measure length to the nearest $\frac{1}{2}$ inch, inch, foot, yard, centimeter, and meter.
15	C	Computation and Estimation	Represent multiplication and division through 10 × 10, using a variety of approaches and models.
16	B	Measurement and Geometry	Tell time to the nearest minute, using analog and digital clocks.
17	A	Number and Number Sense	Compare fractions having like and unlike denominators, using words and symbols (>, <, =, or ≠), with models.
18	C	Computation and Estimation	Represent multiplication and division through 10 × 10, using a variety of approaches and models.
19	10, 14, 28	Patterns, Functions, and Algebra	Identify, describe, create, and extend patterns found in objects, pictures, numbers and tables.
20	20, 32, 44	Computation and Estimation	Create and solve single-step practical problems that involve multiplication and division through 10 x 10.

SOL Mathematics, Practice Test 4, Section 2

Question	Answer	Topic	Mathematics Standard
1	B	Computation and Estimation	Create and solve single-step and multistep practical problems involving sums or differences of two whole numbers, each 9,999 or less.
2	2, 3, 1, 4	Number and Number Sense	Compare fractions having like and unlike denominators, using words and symbols (>, <, =, or ≠), with models.
3	A	Computation and Estimation	Create and solve single-step practical problems that involve multiplication and division through 10 x 10.
4	C	Computation and Estimation	Create and solve single-step and multistep practical problems involving sums or differences of two whole numbers, each 9,999 or less.
5	$\frac{4}{2}, \frac{8}{4}$	Number and Number Sense	Name and write fractions and mixed numbers represented by a model.
6	D	Probability and Statistics	Read and interpret data represented in pictographs and bar graphs.
7	$\frac{3}{6}$ and $\frac{6}{12}$	Number and Number Sense	Compare fractions having like and unlike denominators, using words and symbols (>, <, =, or ≠), with models.
8	Dean: kite Selma: triangle	Measurement and Geometry	Identify and name polygons with 10 or fewer sides.
9	B	Measurement and Geometry	Estimate and measure the distance around a polygon in order to determine its perimeter using U.S. customary and metric units.
10	D	Probability and Statistics	Investigate and describe the concept of probability as a measurement of chance and list possible outcomes for a single event.
11	See Below	Number and Number Sense	Round whole numbers, 9,999 or less, to the nearest ten, hundred, and thousand.
12	48, 54, 60	Patterns, Functions, and Algebra	Identify, describe, create, and extend patterns found in objects, pictures, numbers and tables.
13	5 years	Computation and Estimation	Demonstrate fluency with multiplication facts of 0, 1, 2, 5, and 10.
14	21 square centimeters	Measurement and Geometry	Estimate and count the number of square units needed to cover a given surface in order to determine its area.
15	17 customers	Computation and Estimation	Create and solve single-step and multistep practical problems involving sums or differences of two whole numbers, each 9,999 or less.
16	Jan: bar to 18 Feb: bar to 16 Mar: Bar to 14 $5	Probability and Statistics	Collect, organize, and represent data in pictographs or bar graphs. Read and interpret data represented in pictographs and bar graphs.
17	See Below	Patterns, Functions, and Algebra	Identify, describe, create, and extend patterns found in objects, pictures, numbers and tables.
18	B	Measurement and Geometry	Determine the value of a collection of bills and coins whose total value is $5.00 or less.
19	See Below	Number and Number Sense	Represent fractions and mixed numbers with models and symbols.
20	See Below	Number and Number Sense	Compare and order whole numbers, each 9,999 or less.

Q11.
The number 48 should be plotted on the number line.
Answer: 50
The student should explain how you can tell that the number is closer to 50 than 40.

Scoring Information
Give a total score out of 3.
Give a score of 1 for the number correctly plotted on the number line.
Give a score of 1 for rounding the number correctly.
Give a score out of 1 for the explanation.

Q17.
Answer: 25

The explanation should describe how each number in the pattern is 3 more than the number before it, and that the next number is found by adding 3 to 22.

Scoring Information
Give a total score out of 3.
Give a score of 1 for the correct answer.
Give a score out of 2 for the explanation.

Q19.
The model should have 3 parts of 18 shaded, or 1 part of 6 shaded, as shown below.

 or

Answer: $\frac{1}{6}$

Scoring Information
Give a total score out of 3.
Give a score of 2 for the correct shading.
Give a score of 1 for the correct answer.

Q20.
146 and 164

The explanation should refer to the place value of the numbers. It may describe how the number with the lowest value should be in the hundreds place.

Scoring Information
Give a total score out of 4.
Give a score of 1 for each correct number.
Give a score out of 2 for the explanation.

Get to Know Our Product Range

Mathematics

Practice Test Books
Practice sets and practice tests will prepare students for the state tests.

Quiz Books
Focused individual quizzes cover every math skill one by one.

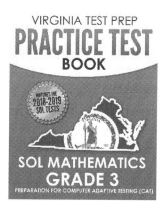  

Reading

Practice Test Books
Practice sets and practice tests will prepare students for the state tests.

Reading Skills Workbooks
Short passages and question sets will develop and improve reading comprehension skills.

Writing

Writing Skills Workbooks
Students write narratives, essays, and opinion pieces, and write in response to passages.

Persuasive and Narrative Writing Workbooks
Guided workbooks teach all the skills required to write effective narratives and opinion pieces.

Language

Language Quiz Books
Focused quizzes cover spelling, grammar, writing conventions, and vocabulary.

Revising and Editing Workbooks
Students improve language and writing skills by identifying and correcting errors.

Language Skills Workbooks
Exercises on specific language skills including idioms, synonyms, and homophones.

 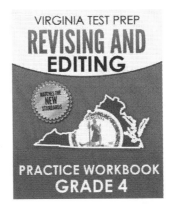 

http://www.testmasterpress.com

Made in the USA
Middletown, DE
05 February 2023

24130498R00080